David Wojtowycz presents

# Animal ABC

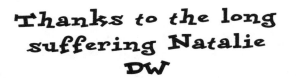

Thanks to the long
suffering Natalie
DW

ISBN 0-439-20621-9

Copyright © 1999 by David Wojtowycz. All rights reserved.
Published by Scholastic Inc., 555 Broadway, New York, NY 10012,
by arrangement with Sterling Publishers. SCHOLASTIC and associated logos
are trademarks and/or registered trademarks of Scholastic Inc.

12 11 10 9 8 7 6 5 4                                                4 5/0

Printed in the U.S.A.                            08

First Scholastic printing, October 2000

David Wojtowycz presents

# Animal ABC

SCHOLASTIC INC.

New York   Toronto   London   Auckland   Sydney
Mexico City   New Delhi   Hong Kong

T 7379

**B b** is for . . .
ballet-dancing
bumble-bee

**Dd** is for . . . driving dragonfly

**F f** is for . . .

fire-
fighting
flea

**G g** is for . . .

gardening gorilla

# Hh

is for ...
handsome
hippo

# I i is for . . .

itchy
iguana

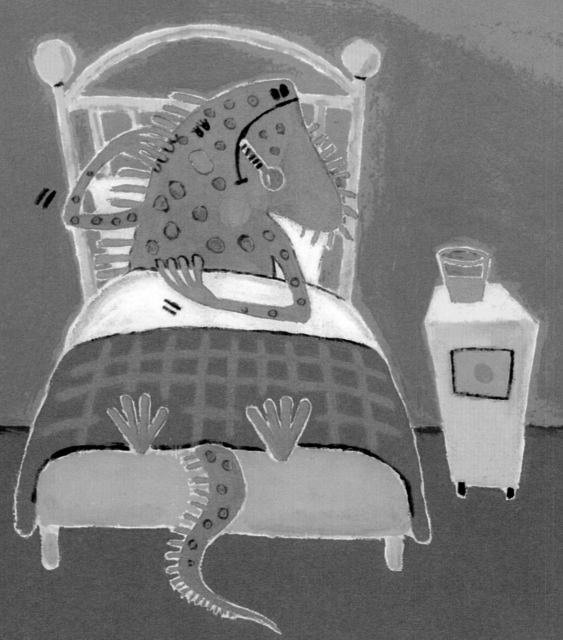

**J j** is for . . .
jet-propelled
jack-
rabbit

**K k** is for . . .

king-sized kiwi

L l is for . . .

leaping lemming

# Mm

is for ...

## magical monkey

Nn is for....

nautical
nightingale

P p

is for . . .
parading
piranhas

**R r** is for . . .

roller-
skating
rooster

U u is for . . . undercover urchin

V v is for . . .

vacuum-cleaning vulture

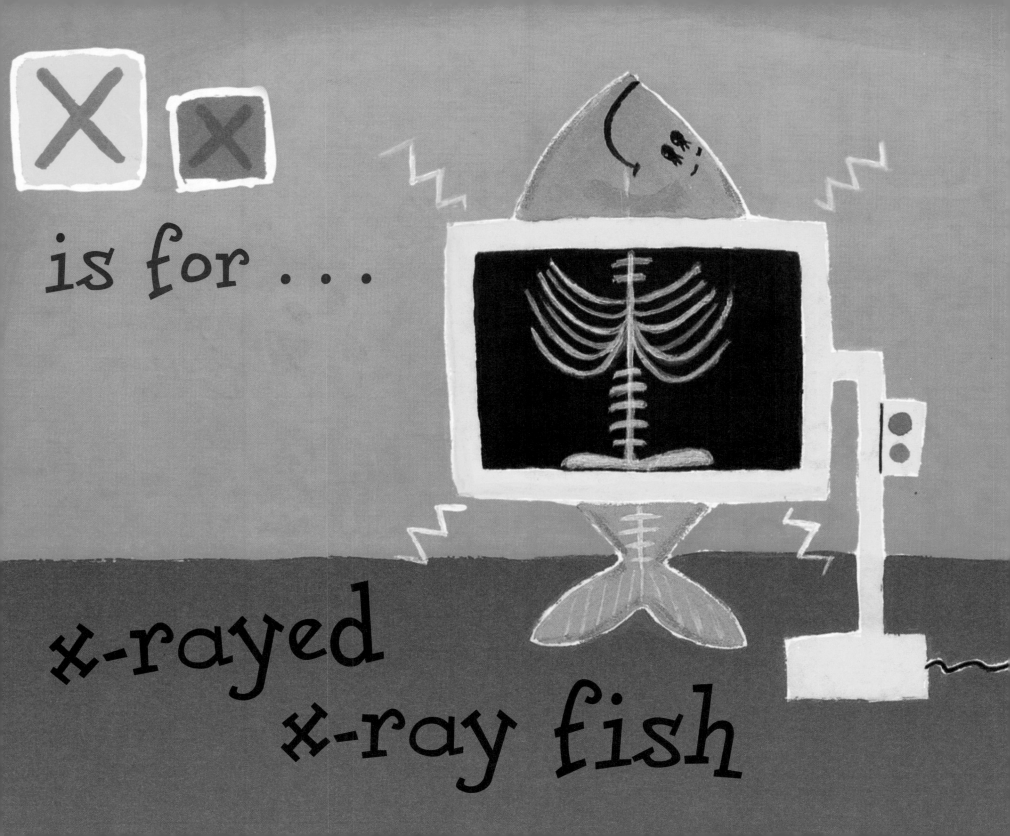

X x is for . . .

x-rayed x-ray fish

Y y

is for . . .

yodelling
yak

**Z z** is for . . .
zig-zag
zebra

# Aa

Aardvark

# Bb

Bumble-bee

# Cc

Cow

# Dd

Dragonfly

# Ii

Iguana

# Jj

Jack-rabbit

# Kk

Kiwi

# Ll

Lemming

# Mm

Monkey

# Ss

Snake

# Tt

Toad

# Uu

Urchin

# Vv

Vulture

Elephant

Flea

Gorilla

Hi

Nightingale

Octopus

Piranha

Quail

R

Whale

X-ray fish

Yak

Ze